bathroom
essentials

MAGGIE STEVENSON

bathroom
essentials

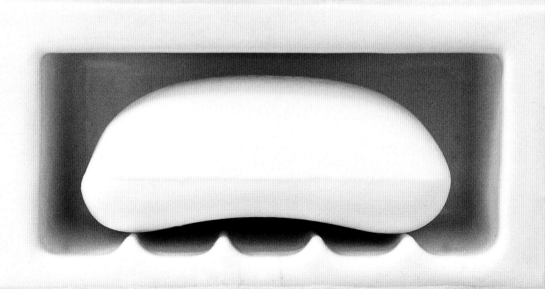

RYLAND
PETERS
& SMALL
LONDON NEW YORK

Designer Emilie Ekström
Senior editor Henrietta Heald
Picture research Emily Westlake
Production Deborah Wehner
Art director Gabriella Le Grazie
Publishing director Alison Starling

First published in the USA
in 2004 by Ryland Peters & Small, Inc.
519 Broadway
5th Floor
New York, NY 10012
www.rylandpeters.com
10 9 8 7 6 5 4 3 2 1

Text copyright © Maggie Stevenson 2004
Design and photographs copyright
© Ryland Peters & Small 2004

Printed and bound in China.

Library of Congress Cataloging-in-Publication Data
Stevenson, Maggie.
  Bathroom essentials / Maggie Stevenson.
    p. cm.
Includes index.
  ISBN 1-84172-606-0
  1. Bathrooms. 2. Interior decoration. I. Title.
NK2117.B33S74 2004
747.7'8--dc22
                                        2003019251

contents

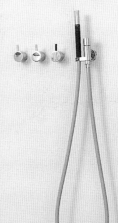

getting the

elements right

planning the space

The most efficient way to begin the planning process is to define the role of your new bathroom. Will it be a connecting or family bathroom? Is it likely to be used by more than one person at a time? Will any of those using the bathroom be very young or old and infirm? Do you want it to double as a dressing room? Do you like to bathe quickly or in a leisurely way? Do you need storage only for toiletries or for towels and cleaning products as well? Think about style, too. Do you favor a contemporary or traditional look? Does the design need to integrate with an adjoining room? The answers to these questions and others like them will help you to decide your priorities.

Above This narrow corridor of a bathroom relies on glass, mirror, and dramatic lighting to push back its boundaries. The working area is defined by its pale limestone wall and floor, and clear glass partitions separate the zones of activity.

Left A custom-made shower makes clever use of a confined space in this tiny internal bathroom. The curved shape eliminates the need for a shower door, and its glass brick construction allows light to enter from an adjoining room.

Opposite, left and right This long, narrow bathroom has been made into a visually squarer, more comfortable space by fitting a shower cubicle across one end wall and building the tub into a raised platform at the other. Light emanating from above and below the wall behind the basin focuses attention at the center of the room and adds to the impression of greater width.

The basic fixtures for a conventional bathroom are a sink, toilet, and tub, but there are many variations, and your choice will depend on the style you want, your budget, and the size of the room. In a small bathroom the tub could be exchanged for a shower enclosure to save space—or, for a feeling of openness, the room could be designed as a fully waterproofed wet-room. If you want both a tub and shower, the choice is between separate fixtures or an overbath shower. In some countries, every well-appointed bathroom contains a bidet, while in others it is an optional extra. Generally, top-quality fixtures with designer labels are expensive, but there are plenty of good-looking alternatives in affordable lines.

To see whether your fixtures will fit into the available space, draw a scale floor plan of the room and elevations of each wall on graph paper, then cut out cardboard shapes representing

the fixtures to the same scale (manufacturers' brochures give exact sizes). On the floor plan and elevations, mark all permanent features such as windows and doors, and place the cutouts on the plan, moving them around to find a good layout. Tubs need a strip at least 36in (90cm) wide beside them to let bathers step out and dry themselves; showers need a space 28in (70cm) wide. Sinks need 28in (70cm) in front and 8in (20cm) at each side; the toilet and bidet need 24in (60cm) in front and 8in (20cm) at the sides.

In a room used by one person at a time, access areas can be overlapped slightly, but rooms used simultaneously by two or more people need extra space. While arranging the fixtures, refer to the elevations to identify any conflict with doors, windows, or radiators. To accommodate awkward layouts, doors can be re-hung or moved, and radiators moved or replaced by underfloor heating.

- Spend time getting your plans right. **Even small changes** like installing a shaver socket or an extractor fan **will be disruptive** if they are made later.

- Bathroom **fixtures come in many shapes and sizes**; if you are planning a small or awkwardly shaped room, look at as many brochures as you can.

- If you want a chair, cabinet, or other freestanding furniture in the room, allow for it **at the planning stage**.

- Pipework collects dirt and looks unsightly, so **hide it behind boxed baseboards**, false walls, or some other form of ducting.

Above and left Open shelves and a console vanity unit leave the floor area in this bathroom uncluttered and easy to clean.
Opposite, above Designed for busy mornings, this compact shower room has a long basin that two people can use at the same time. A flanking wall screens an open shower enclosure from the door.
Opposite, below A false wall constructed along one side of the room neatly hides the tank for a back-to-the-wall toilet and the plumbing for a shower.

Above Thick tinted glass forms a sleek countertop with integral circular bowls. Super stylish, it is also practical, with no joints where dirt and minerals can lodge.

Right and opposite, left Visually as well as physically weighty, the gray-brown mussel limestone covering most of the surfaces in this room is offset by expanses of white. On the horizontal, the stone is polished to show off the subtleties of its color and texture, but on the vertical planes it is has been given narrow, regular grooves for textural and tonal contrast.

Opposite, right This superior form of duckboarding surrounding a sunken tub lets water drain through it.

surfaces, flooring, & lighting

The floor and walls form the background against which fixtures, furniture, and accessories are seen. Since they make up such a large part of the picture, the materials covering them have a major influence on the style of a room; similar or complementary materials are likely to be used for the countertops, tub surround, and other hardworking surfaces. Bathrooms require two distinct types of lighting: general all-over illumination and task lighting.

The ideal flooring for a conventional bathroom is water-tolerant, easy to clean, slip-resistant, and warm to the touch. Vinyl, rubber, and cork have all these qualities, but tile, stone, glass, wood, and even carpet are suitable floor coverings provided they are chosen and used with care. Hard materials such as tile, stone, and glass are often used in modern settings, but they are cold and potentially slippery when wet.

Wood and carpet may be the least water-tolerant materials, but they are comfortable to walk on and look luxurious. Unless you choose the kind specifically designed for bathrooms, laminated wood flooring may swell and distort in a damp environment, and solid lumber requires careful sealing to protect against splinters and watermarks. Duckboarding and painted floorboards remain comparatively unscathed by water and can safely be used in adult bathrooms where the floor does not get too wet.

The choice of wall treatments suitable for bathrooms is almost limitless, provided the wet areas are properly protected. Continuous surfaces are often chosen for a contemporary scheme to give a sophisticated, seamless look, and for small spaces that appear all the more cramped if the walls are fragmented into a patchwork of textures and colors. Materials suitable for creating this all-over look include ceramic or glass tiles and mosaic and natural and synthetic stone, all of which are comparatively expensive but long-lasting,

Above Terra cotta, hardwood, rubber, and porcelain are all suitable flooring materials for wet areas and make strong foundations for specific bathroom styles. Terra-cotta tiles have a robust look and natural color that warms country bathrooms; wooden boards are now the first choice for a smart urban setting; resilient rubber is a practical choice for a family bathroom; while porcelain offers a variety of size, shape and color on a grand scale.
Opposite, right Random mosaic, corrugated vinyl roofing, and sheet vinyl flooring are inexpensive surface elements that combine harmoniously to create a practical and colorful bathroom.

Left Softwood is not generally recommended for bathroom flooring, but exposed floorboards, naturally ventilated from beneath and painted to provide some protection from moisture, are serviceable and have a certain rustic charm. A cotton runner placed alongside the tub gives further protection from water where it is most needed, and is a soft surface to step onto.

waterproof, and easy to clean. In traditional bathrooms and lower-budget installations, paint and wallpaper are decorative options for all walls other than those in the shower enclosure; if a uniform look is required, surfaces immediately around the bathtub and basin can be protected with clear glass or acrylic panels or plain matching tiles.

Wood paneling is an option for the walls of both traditional and modern bathrooms. In the bathrooms of period or country homes, painted tongue-and-groove wainscoting or fielded paneling covering the lower part of the wall may be continued around the room; they will withstand normal levels of bathroom moisture, though not the direct spray of a

Above Drawn from nature, the floor in this bathroom is made from beach pebbles set in concrete, while the wall is clad with the pale, blond stems of bamboo.
Left Inexpensive plywood tiles take on a glamorous look when laid diamond fashion and studded with "keystones" of black-stained ply. Lacquer applied in several layers not only protects the wood from moisture but enhances its golden tones and gives it a satin sheen.

Below The tough industrial aesthetic of concrete is an interesting and unexpected contrast to sleek, domesticated materials such as lacquer and mirror glass. Custom-fabricated, it must be sealed before use.
Right Dark, handsome and expensive, iroko wood paneling remains unblemished by water. Lightly oiled to maintain its rich color, the wood gives the room a sense of luxury and permanence.
Far right Porcelain tiles, whose color and texture recall polished limestone, form a waterproof panel that can be distinguished from the wall only by its reflectivity. The mosaic bath panel adds further surface interest, but allows no color to intrude on this neutral scheme.

shower. Natural or oiled hardwood, such as iroko or merbau, is the modern alternative. Dark tropical woods resist water to a degree, but will fade if not regularly oiled.

Smooth, pannelled surfaces are easier to clean than tiles or mosaic, which eventually accumulate grime in their grouted joints. The most popular of these are limestone, marble, granite, Corian, and glass; in urban homes, industrial materials like concrete and sheet metals may be added to the list. All of them are hard-wearing, but extra care must be taken with limestone and marble, which can be marked by acidic cleaners and cosmetics, and badly damaged by cleaners that contain mineral-deposit remover.

As in other rooms in the home, the best general light in a bathroom is provided by daylight. In most bathrooms, you can maximize this by keeping window treatments simple, but in windowless internal bathrooms more radical measures will be necessary, such as replacing sections of the wall with glass bricks or obscured glass panels to allow light from an adjoining room to pass through.

After dark and on gray wintry days, a central ceiling light, downlights recessed into the ceiling, or wall fixtures give even all-over light, leaving no gloomy spots in the room.

Bathroom task lighting—for activities such as shaving and applying makeup—centers on the mirror and should be directed so that it shines on your face. A pair of lights placed at the sides of the mirror will give a clear, virtually shadow-free light; the light sources may either be separate wall-mounted fixtures or incorporated into the mirror itself.

Above A curve of obscured glass separates a shower area from a living space. Its frosted finish diffuses, and maximizes, the light passing through.
Left This dark, concrete-lined shower enclosure is studded at regular intervals with pale circular tiles that reflect light from the overhead fixture.
Right Light wood paneling gives a small bathroom a sophisticated look, and a large, unframed mirror increases the sense of space.
Opposite, above right A combination of hardwood decking and white mosaic tiles provides safe, moisture-resistant surfaces around a sunken bathtub.
Opposite, below right Loose-laid beach pebbles interspersed with uplighters form a natural border for a wooden boardwalk floor.

- Stone is **a wonderful all-purpose surfacing material**, but in bathrooms it must be sealed.

- Industrial surfaces such as sheet metal, concrete, and rubber create **an urban look**.

- Glass and mirror introduce glamour and **a sense of light and space**.

- Basins set into countertops are practical as well as good-looking; they can be made from **natural or synthetic stone, steel, or glass**.

- Floor lights, spotlights, and **concealing lights** add drama to a lighting scheme.

- For safety, all light fixtures should be **rated for bathroom use**.

fixtures & appliances

There are fixtures to suit every kind of bathroom. To pick your way through the bathroom maze, first identify your priorities and your personal style. Make a wish list of your ideal fixtures, then edit it down to match your budget, lifestyle, and the space available. If you don't know what style you want, gather bathroom brochures, books, and magazines, and mark the pictures that appeal—you'll soon see if you lean toward modern or traditional shapes.

Above A mixer faucet set into the marble top of a low partition wall at the foot of a bathtub projects into the tub to a lesser degree than it would if it were wall- or rim-mounted, allowing for more comfortable bathing in a smaller than standard-size bathtub.

Right This custom-made glass basin—cantilevered from the wall with no visible means of support—is designed for washing under running water. Slim, shallow, and with a backward-sloping base, it is long enough for two people to use at the same time, but it has a single plugless waste, so there is no possibility of water overflowing. Uncomplicated wall-mounted faucets add to the minimalist effect.

Above and top Countertop basins come in various shapes to suit the style and size of room. Faucets to fill them should be wall-mounted or extra-tall deck fixtures.

Left A traditional fixed shower head provides no choice of invigorating spray patterns— simply a heavy, drenching rain of water, with separate cross-head handles to control temperature and flow.

Popular bathtub materials include cast iron, enameled steel, pressed acrylic, and cast synthetics. Cast iron is heavy and stable with a lustrous porcelain enameled finish; enameled steel is lighter, and pressed acrylic lighter still. Cast synthetics mimic cast iron, but are lighter and warm to the touch.

Most built-in tubs are rectangular and available in a range of standard sizes, but corner baths and tapered baths are an option in small or awkwardly shaped rooms. Freestanding bathtubs made from cast iron or cast synthetics come in modern oval shapes as well as the traditional rolltop form. While antique-style tubs stand on decorative legs, the modern ones have chunky wooden legs and rest on the floor, or on wooden or stone stands. To make the tub the main feature in the room, consider custom tubs made from stone, wood, or stainless steel, or an antique tub in ceramic or copper.

In Europe as well as America, a shower is now regarded as an essential piece of bathroom equipment, in addition to, or instead of, a bathtub. A shower enclosure is ideal, but if space is tight, an overbath shower is a practical alternative.

Above The sprays from these twin showerheads overlap to give an even coverage within the large, rectangular shower enclosure. The exposed pipework supplying them is so neatly stapled along the ceiling that it makes minimal impact on the décor.

Right Although the bathtub is similar in shape to a comfortable Victorian rolltop version, instead of having decorative cast-iron legs, this contemporary copy rests on angular limestone cradles, giving it a cleaner, more streamlined look that is more appropriate in a modern bathroom.

Shower enclosures consist of a shower tray and a waterproof surround. Usually, the shower tray is made from steel or a rigid synthetic material. The surround can be simply an alcove tiled or faced with stone or some other waterproof material, an enclosure formed by two glass or acrylic panels, or a self-contained shower cubicle. The door may be hinged, but, to make best use of space, choose bi-fold, sliding, or pivoting doors that open without encroaching on the room. The fixtures that deliver the shower spray draw on stored hot water or heat the water as needed. Showers that use stored water offer the

Top, left to right Supataps with the handle and spout made as a single unit have a retro charm. A shower head with tiny projections directs the water in fine jets to give an invigorating spray. A modern freestanding bathtub is filled from a simple chrome spout rising from the floor and curving smoothly over the rim.

Above, left to right The combination of a fixed wide shower head and a hand-held shower allows a choice between a relaxing overhead drench or targeted showering. Separate controls for temperature and flow allow you to establish your ideal setting. A three-hole faucet has separate controls for hot and cold water.

greatest choice of fixtures, including fixed-head and hand-held sprays. More powerful showers that incorporate body sprays, foot sprays, and deluge sprays may need a pump to increase water pressure.

Washbasins are many and varied. The choice is between a pedestal basin that rests on a ceramic column which hides the pipework, a cantilevered wall-mounted basin, a vanity basin mounted under or integrated into a countertop, a console basin that rests on or is built into a decorative stand, and a countertop basin, rectangular, oval or round, which stands on a shelf or tabletop. Most basins are made from glazed ceramic, but other materials such as glass, stone, cast synthetics, stainless steel, and wood are becoming more widely available.

Toilets and bidets are floor-standing or wall-mounted. Ceramic is the most prevalent material for these fixtures, although stainless steel is sometimes preferred for bathrooms with an industrial aesthetic.

Faucets are available in a wide range of traditional, classic, and contemporary designs to match the baths and basins they fill. Finishes include chrome, nickel, gold, and various antique effects, and the most popular configurations are separate hot and cold pillar faucets, three-hole mixers with handles to control hot and cold water and a separate spout, and the monobloc or single lever mixer, which controls the temperature and flow of the water.

Left The tank and pipework for this wall-mounted bidet and toilet are hidden in ducting, and the fixtures are hung clear of the floor.
Below A valve-operated flush does not have the approval of every water authority, but it works efficiently and takes up less space than a tank.
Right Similar in style to the Belfast kitchen sink, this shallow basin is a practical shape for wet shaving and washing.

• Before you buy a large bathtub made from **cast iron, stone, or wood**, check that the floor will bear the combined weight of the tub and water.

• If you need extra storage, choose **a vanity basin with cupboard space below**. These can be found in contemporary and traditional styles.

• In a small bathroom, **a shower cubicle with a sliding or folding door** will open without colliding with other fixtures.

• Unless it will be used just for hand rinsing, buy the **largest bathroom basin** you can accommodate. It will contain splashes and allow for more **energetic washing**.

storage, furniture, & accessories

A well-ordered bathroom is more conducive to relaxing, bathing, and grooming than one that is littered with half-used shampoo bottles and damp towels. Good storage will bring the clutter under control. Built-in cupboards and vanity units generally provide bathroom storage, but there are situations where freestanding cabinets, rods, racks, and containers are a useful addition or a practical alternative.

Left and above Glass shelves make good use of a space formerly occupied by a fireplace and its chimney. By day, the shelves' transparency contributes to the room's open, airy atmosphere, and at night, lights recessed into the top of the alcove beam through all the shelves, making a glowing display of the objects on them.

Opposite The bank of birchwood cabinets lining one side of this bathroom has twin washbasins mounted under its thick carrara marble countertop along with a series of cabinets and drawers. Raising the unit on short chrome legs makes the floor area seem larger and the unit itself less bulky.

Bathroom storage should combine open shelves or glazed cabinets for display and closed storage for those items you would prefer to hide. In bathrooms where space or budget is limited, the traditional bathroom cabinet mounted on the wall above the basin provides basic storage for essentials.

Floor-standing cabinets, trolleys, and shelf units are a useful addition to most unfitted bathrooms. Cabinets are generally low and square, with a cupboard, drawers, or a combination of the two. Storage trolleys are designed for maneuverability and may be equipped with brakes so they can be parked wherever they are needed. These mobile units range in style from mesh or polished metal trolleys to contemporary wooden designs and rustic painted cupboards.

Freestanding shelf units are efficient space savers. Like cabinets, they come in many materials. Glass shelves must be made from special toughened glass and have polished edges; they are ideal for small spaces since they allow light to pass through. Painted shelves are practical and easy to refresh with a new coat of paint when they begin to look shabby. Wire mesh is well suited to shelves, but the mesh will not contain spilt liquids. Although wooden shelves intended for bathroom use will be protected with a durable finish, furniture that has been designed for other rooms may not be so resistant to bathroom products. Even in the smallest bathroom, space can be found to

This page Built-in cupboards and drawers turn unused spaces into useful storage. Stained plywood drawers fill the space under a concrete vanity unit; silky, pale birch cabinets and drawers are recessed into the wall; while a huge armoire with imposing paneled oak doors slots neatly into an alcove.

Opposite Simple and relatively inexpensive ideas can solve specific storage problems. An antique shelf set high on the wall at the foot end of the tub holds fresh towels within easy reach of the person using the overbath shower. A wicker hamper stores towels and spare toilet paper, and a purpose-made wall- or door-mounted rack keeps magazines handy.

hang wall shelves. Ready-made units are simply screwed to the wall, but cut-to-size shelves will fit any available space.

Towel rods keep towels neat and allow them to air after use. Unheated towel rods are made of wood, plastic, or metal, and can be wall-mounted or floor-standing. The wall-mounted types take the form of a ring or a single or double straight rod supported on brackets in a design to match other wall-mounted bathroom accessories. Rings for hand towels are placed beside a basin or bidet, but straight rods are large enough to hold a bath towel. Floor-standing rods usually have more than one rod and allow several towels to dry at once.

Right Invaluable in a bathroom where shelf space is limited, this slim vertical rod, reaching from floor to ceiling, supports towels, toothbrush holder, and a swing-arm magnifying mirror that is adjustable to various levels.

Below left Every shower enclosure needs somewhere to rest the soap or sponge, and this minimal stainless-steel holder is in keeping with the urban style of its concrete and mosaic surroundings.

Below right An alcove, recessed into the wall at eye level and tiled with the same mosaic, is roomy enough to hold a selection of hair-care and shower preparations.

Individual wall-mounted holders for soaps, sponges, shaving equipment, toothbrushes, and toilet-paper holders can be mounted where they are needed. In the shower, corner shelves and tiered sets of wire baskets hold shower gel and shampoos within easy reach.

Most wall-mounted racks and holders are screwed to the wall, but in areas with tiled or glass walls, fixtures that are attached by suction pads are easier to install.

Bath racks that rest like a bridge across the bathtub hold all the necessary equipment for bathing, and some luxurious models have integral book rests, candle holders, or a shaving mirror.

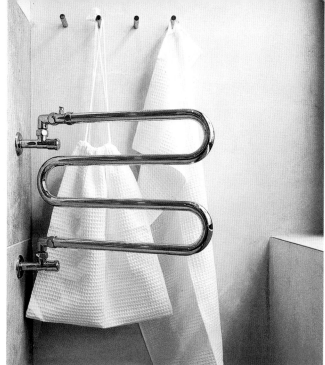

A laundry basket helps keep the room neat. Towels and clothes can be dropped into it the moment they are discarded. Some laundry bins are lined with a fabric bag that can be detached, allowing the laundry to be carried straight to the washing machine.

In most bathrooms, furnishings are limited to the essentials, but if you add a chair, the atmosphere immediately becomes more relaxed and inviting. In a large, well-ventilated bathroom decorated in traditional or country style, an upholstered armchair brings comfort and a touch of luxury, but in a smaller space, light, moisture-resistant wicker or loom is a better choice. In a modern bathroom, a

- A humid atmosphere makes textiles musty, so if you store towels or clothing in a bathroom, **keep it well ventilated**.

- Edit your collection of hair and bath products regularly and **keep on show only those in regular use**.

- Built-in cupboards and shelves **make the best use of space** in an awkwardly shaped bathroom.

- **Fit narrow shelves** in preference to wider ones. They take up less space, look sleek, and the contents can be **seen at a glance**.

- Make sure there are **enough towel rods**. Damp towels piled on top of each other will never dry. In addition to a heated rod, fit hanging pegs and wall-mounted rods **where towels can dry naturally**.

shapely plastic chair produced by one of the modern makers will be impervious to water and contribute to the contemporary style. Bathrooms too small for a chair generally have room for a stool or folding café chair.

The extra surfaces and storage provided by a small table, chest of drawers, or small cupboard are not, strictly speaking, essential in a bathroom, but if you are aiming for a softer, more lived-in look than pared-down functionalism, they are a worthwhile addition.

A small table or cabinet placed alongside the tub makes a suitable place to put your book, a drink, and the radio while you indulge in a relaxing bath, and a chest of drawers with a mirror hung above it will serve as an attractive dressing table.

Above Magnifying mirrors are needed for tasks that require a close-up view; one that tilts and swivels is the most versatile.

Above left Wall-mounted shelves and holders are necessary adjuncts to a traditional pedestal basin that has limited space for essentials.

Left A bamboo stool is useful as a seat or surface and can withstand the moist atmosphere.

Far left The narrow shelf that runs the length of this bathroom is a valuable storage space; to avoid a cluttered effect, the items on it are arranged in neat groups.

Opposite Designed like a locker room, the walls of this dressing room are lined with cupboards of various sizes and open shelves.

putting it

together

Right A semi-sunken bathtub screened by a low, toughened-glass panel barely impacts on the space in this small bathroom. Wall-mounted fixtures let light flow uninterrupted around the room.

Below Unusually for a shower enclosure, the walls, rendered with the waterproof plaster used to line swimming pools, are slightly gritty to the touch, but the slate floor and reinforced-glass shelves offer a smooth contrast.

contemporary

The bathroom lends itself well to modern style. Its cool, smooth surfaces, sculptural fixtures, and highly engineered plumbing combine to create a capsule environment of calm and order that is, for many of us, impossible to maintain with any success elsewhere in the home.

Above Hard surfacing need not mean a cold and spartan look. A large tub and even larger shower area lined with creamy limestone and frosted glass, carefully lit to dramatic effect, create a warm and indulgent bathroom.

Left Color in a monochromatic scheme or a familiar material used in an unusual way make an essentially formal design memorable. Here, the unexpected element is the countertop. Made from blue glass with twin integral washbasins, the surface is raised above a bank of plain, white cabinets, leaving a shelf between the two. Light passing through the tinted glass illuminates the space beneath with an eerie glow.

The pioneers of the contemporary look were in search of simplicity to counter the complexity of modern life—and they turned to natural materials, naked and unadorned, to create it. Their theory worked. A visually quiet space undoubtedly has restorative powers, and although at first the materials and fixtures needed to create it were expensive and readily available only to architects and designers, they have now come within reach of a wider public.

Surfaces that have the right aesthetic credentials for this look include natural materials such as hardwood and stone, and products such as brick, metal, and concrete that have been used in the building industry for generations but were rarely visible in interiors. Add to these glass and modern man-made surfacing materials such as Corian and Lucite, and the scope of contemporary style broadens to encompass a wide range of decorating options.

One of the most recent developments in contemporary bathrooms is the bolder use of color. Previously, color was limited to a natural palette based on the raw materials used for the décor, but gradually mosaic tiles—a cheaper surfacing

Left Metallic wallpapers inject light and drama into a dark bathroom; this one, depicting iconic film stars, adds a touch of glamour.
Above left Hanging a single vibrant picture can send shockwaves through the polite elegance of a dark monochromatic scheme.
Far left Many modern bathrooms incorporate natural materials, but those that include man-made surfaces are more colorful and vigorous. The color in this shower room is at its most conspicuous in the transparent acrylic basin surround and shower screen.

material than stone or wood and available in shimmering, watery pastels that complement the natural tones—were added to give gentle contrast. More intense colors have followed in the form of synthetic surfaces and glass tiles, the latter being available in slip-resistant varieties for floors as well as walls.

Finding appliances, faucets, and showers in contemporary style has never been easier. The seminal designs of well-known architects and industrial designers will always be the purists' first choice, but the mass-market lines they have inspired and the functional no-frills fixtures produced for the building trade make acceptable and affordable substitutes. Large, focal-point bathtubs made from stone, resin, or wood, countertop basins in ceramic, glass, steel, or stone, deceptively simple faucets and wall-mounted toilets and bidets all contribute to the modern look.

Above The design of some modern bathrooms has become formulaic with the same materials and fixtures appearing in different permutations. A uniquely personal effect that is no less current in style is achieved by combining materials in unusual partnerships. This bathroom mixes wood veneer, aluminum, glass, and ceramic tiles in an unusually muscular scheme.
Left Slate cut into thin tiles is suitable for both walls and floors, but because the stone is a dense, dark gray, rooms where it is used extensively must be brightly lit.

simplicity and clean lines . . .

If you need to partition the space in a bathroom, use **glass bricks or panels—** clear or frosted—to allow **light to flood through**.

Remember that **wood, stone, and concrete** all need to be sealed to make them water-resistant.

Mosaic or glass tiles or synthetic surfacing **materials** can be used to introduce color.

Appliances, showers, and faucets in **simple shapes** and wall-mounted toilets with concealed tanks all add to **the streamlined look**.

If you have the budget, a custom-made **countertop with an integral washbasin** is a sophisticated alternative to undermounted bowls.

for modern elegance

country

Luxury and indulgence are present in the typical country-style bathroom—but in the uncomplicated form of thick, laundry-roughened towels, lavender-scented bath water, and a window with a green and pleasant view.

Above Antique fairs and sale rooms are the places to look for old bathroom fixtures such as this enameled basin. Before you buy, check carefully for cracks and chips, which cannot be successfully repaired.

Right Painted wood paneling, a carpet on the floor, and pictures on the wall give this bathroom a relaxed, homey feel. The modern bathtub, raised on chunky turned wood feet and placed alongside a vintage washbasin, adapts well to its traditional surroundings.

Above Few modern basins are as pretty as this Victorian one with its floral transfer decoration. Modern reproductions are available, but they never accurately replicate the deep, inky, indigo blue that makes the original patterns unique.

Left The terrazzo floor, cast-iron tub, and tiled walls have given good service for more than fifty years. The décor still looks fresh, and the addition of a pleated shade at the window and an industrial-style enameled light fixture give the room a cared-for look that does not detract from its retro charm.

Many bathrooms in traditional country homes
have been converted from spare bedrooms,
and often have enough space to allow a
more imaginative layout than is possible in
a modern bathroom. If they are retained,
built-in cupboards, window seats, alcoves,
and other features of the original room add
character. A smaller bathroom, built as an
extension or squeezed into space partitioned
from a large bedroom or landing, will need
clever decoration to give it style.

Suitable reclaimed and reproduction
fixtures come in a variety of shapes, but
if your aim is to create a bathroom that
is visually embedded in its surroundings,
choose only those that match the status
of the building. Victorian or Edwardian

Left and far left Typical elements of country style include the stripped-pine door, traditional shower, fabric curtain, and chunky wooden shelf.
Below Small details have a big impact and these old enamel pots labeled for "soap" and "sand" reinforce the traditional look.
Opposite, top Old and new come together in this vanity stand made by plumbing a modern basin into a painted antique chest.
Opposite, below left A sauna is part of everyday life in northern Europe, but still regarded as a luxury farther south. As the temperature rises, the wood of the walls and benches fills the air with its resinous scent.
Opposite, below right A porcelain-handled spray distinguishes this traditional bath/shower mixer.

sanitaryware, perhaps with floral decoration, is an appropriate choice for larger country houses, while in a modest country cottage, simple fixtures in designs from the 1920s or 1930s would be more suitable. Barns and other converted farm buildings are, by definition, modern, but fixtures in plain shapes are a good match for their pared-down character.

The bathtub is the dominant feature of a country bathroom. A rolltop tub has the right vintage look and is impressive enough to stand in the center of a large bathroom. In a smaller space, a standard tub placed along a wall and boxed in with tongue-and-groove paneling has a suitably nostalgic feel.

Ceramic tiles and painted wood are good choices for wall and floor coverings in a traditional setting. Plain white or cream rectangular wall tiles set brick-fashion have a retro look, but square tiles taken to eye level and edged with a narrow black border or a patchwork of patterned Victorian tiles would also work well. Tiles and wood are also ideal for flooring. For a traditional look, create a checkered effect with black and white tiles, or scrub the floorboards and leave them bare.

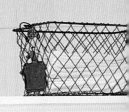

a new life for old things and . . .

Choose fixtures for **visual appeal**. A console washbasin with decorative **ceramic or metal legs** is a pretty alternative to an urban vanity unit.

Reproduction bathtubs and basins take on **an authentic look** when equipped with antique faucets.

Ceramic jugs, **enamel mugs**, and other finds from bric-a-brac stalls make bathroom accessories with **the right period charm**.

Pale, printed cotton curtains, a snowy linen blind, or white-painted shutters all **filter the light** and give privacy.

If you need more storage, **search sale rooms or antique fairs** for cupboards or chests of drawers.

a breath of country air

Left and opposite The space to put a bathroom suite must sometimes be stolen from the bedroom itself. Less expensive than building a solid wall between the two zones, frosted-glass panels screening the washbasin and overbath shower areas give privacy where it is needed and contain the wet areas. The use of translucent materials and an open-plan layout means that the bathing area does not feel cramped nor the bedroom too much reduced.

Below Building a shower under the roof slope in a remodeled attic makes sense as long as there is full head height in the place where the person using it will be standing. A larger floor area—however low the ceiling at the farthest point—will give a feeling of space within the enclosure.

small bathrooms

Lack of space is so common in a bathroom that it barely registers as a design challenge, but now that bathing is an act of self-indulgence as much as a daily routine, the room must reflect its dual role. A well-planned layout, careful use of color, and some ingenious design tricks will stretch the limits of a compact room, making it seem comfortable but never cramped.

A combination of pale colors, clear glass, and reflective surfaces can create an illusion of space in a small bathroom. Moreover, improved plumbing and specially designed fixtures mean there is no reason why compactness should preclude efficiency and elegance. The bathroom in a good hotel demonstrates how successful a small bathroom can be. Rarely larger than is absolutely necessary, it contains all the essentials, yet still manages to convey a sense of luxury through its streamlined layout and use of top-quality fixtures and surfaces. The home bathroom differs from this only in its need to include adequate storage.

In a compact space, cabinets and drawers are preferable to open shelves because they allow you to reduce the amount of clutter on view and make good use of otherwise dead areas under the sink, in alcoves, and behind the paneling that conceals tanks and pipework and encloses the bathtub.

The way fixtures are arranged within a room affects how spacious it seems. In addition to making a floor plan, it is worth drawing an elevation of each wall so you can take the height and bulk of the fixtures into account as well as the ground space they occupy. It is tempting to find room for all the fixtures on your wish list, but sometimes the layout works better, and the room feels more open, if you compromise by having an overbath shower instead of a separate shower

Below Hinged doors require space to open, but in this shower room sliding doors have been used on the cabinets as well as the entrance, allowing every little bit of floor space to be put to work.

Opposite, below Barely larger than an average powder room, this tiny shower room relies on good lighting and the pale colors of natural limestone to enhance its modest dimensions. A clear, frameless partition divides the space without visually compartmentalizing it.

Opposite, above Sometimes, because it is usually seen in the context of a larger room, a single imposing piece of furniture creates the illusion of space. Here, a large mirror, a glass door, and white walls balance the dark wooden vanity unit so it does not dominate completely.

enclosure or install a large shower instead of a tub. A less crowded room will feel relaxed, look better, and be more convenient to use.

Visual devices to make a small room seem bigger include allowing light to flow through the space by choosing a frameless shower enclosure glazed with clear reinforced glass— or even abandoning enclosures and partitions altogether in favor of a wet-room where all surfaces are waterproofed. Wall-mounted fixtures make the floor area appear larger, and cabinets or vanity units that are raised on legs have a less bulky look. Even oddly shaped rooms can be made to feel more comfortable. For example, in a tall, narrow space, the perceived height can be reduced by tiling the walls to a level that stops short of the ceiling.

To reduce the apparent length of a long, narrow room, the tub can be placed across its width at one end, and an open shower area across it at the other. Arranging the other fixtures along one wall between them will give an impression of space at the center of the room, which can be accentuated by putting mirrors on opposite sides of the room and hanging a lamp centrally over the area.

One way to give a more streamlined look both inside and outside a bathroom is to replace hinged doors with sliding pocket doors. Unlike track-mounted doors, which side over the wall they open onto, pocket doors are set into double-thickness walls; when open, they disappear into the space between the leaves of the wall.

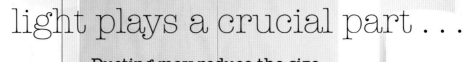

light plays a crucial part . . .

Ducting may reduce the size of the room slightly, but it **conceals pipework** and the toilet tank, giving a neat look, and **storage can be recessed into it**.

Try **decorating the room** entirely in a single color or material. **Continuity** adds to a calm, relaxed atmosphere.

Cool, light colors such as **pale blue, lilac, and aqua** seem to recede, making a room seem larger.

Make use of awkward spaces **in alcoves or under the eaves** for storage or activities that don't require **a full-height ceiling**.

in creating a sense of space

family-friendly

Families are never static, and in a household with young children the bathroom should be flexible enough to adapt as they grow. Get the basics right by providing efficient heating, waterproof surfaces, and robust fixtures that will stand up to the heavy wear they will inevitably receive, and respond to your children's developing tastes by changing the décor and accessories.

Above To prevent children from locking themselves in the bathroom by accident, install latches that can be opened from the outside.
Left An open-plan connecting bathroom is a parents' sanctuary, but for children the chance to bathe in such a luxurious grown-up space is a special treat; a lockable door is essential if you want to keep this personal space private.
Right A few well-chosen accessories can alter the style of a plain white bathroom. A primary-colored shower curtain and toothbrush glass will appeal to younger children and can easily be replaced as their tastes develop.

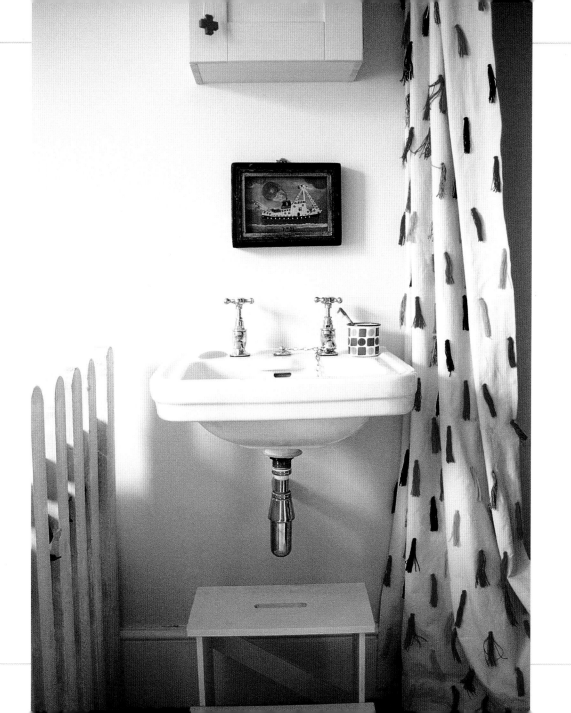

Very young children need help with every aspect of personal care from teeth-brushing to using the toilet, so bathrooms designed for families must have plenty of clear space to allow parent and child to move around easily. The tub in particular needs enough space for a parent to kneel or sit beside it to supervise bathing, read stories, or just discuss the day before helping their child towel dry and put on their pajamas.

When choosing fixtures, opt for a bigger tub—preferably with faucets and plug hole placed centrally—so two children can bathe simultaneously. If there is room, install twin sinks; they will be invaluable when children start school and the whole family needs to leave home at the same time each day.

Walls, floors, and other surfaces should be both safe and practical. Floors must be waterproof, slip-resistant, and warm to the touch. Materials such as rubber, linoleum, cork, and vinyl have the right characteristics and, unlike ceramic tiles, provide a relatively soft landing if accidents do happen.

Left Built-in storage alcoves keep bathtime necessities close at hand.
Below This translucent plastic shower curtain with pockets is used as an ever-changing gallery of family photographs.
Opposite, left A square bathtub, tailored to fit the space, with a ledge all around for toys and toiletries, is large enough to bathe two or three children at once.
Opposite, above right A wide shelf makes a useful changing area for a small baby, and open shelves offer easy-access storage.
Opposite, below right Twin basins save time in the morning rush hour, and mirrored cabinets recessed flush with the wall are less enticing to younger children.

Children tend to splash water around, and wall and surface materials that wipe down easily and won't be damaged by water are ideal. Tiles or special bathroom paints are the most tolerant wall treatments, while laminate, tile, or stone surfaces for shelves and the tops of units are good-looking and robust.

Provide ample storage in the form of pegs to hold towels, bathrobes, and laundry bags; open shelves for things in frequent use such as toiletries; spare towels; baby-changing items and toys; and cabinets—some of them lockable—to keep potentially hazardous cleaning products, medicines, and perfume sprays out of harm's way.

Try color-coding toothbrushes, mugs, and towels to remind children to use only their own personal kit and mount rods lower on the wall to encourage them to hang up towels. Allow early independence by providing sturdy, stable step-stools to give easier access to the sink and toilet.

thoughtful details help to make . . .

Make it **easy for children** to keep the bathroom neat by putting **pegs and rods** at a height they can easily reach.

To reduce the risk of falls, choose **slip-resistant flooring,** mop up spilt liquids, and keep the floor clear of toys, step-stools, and **other obstacles**.

Choose a bright color scheme. In case the décor outlasts your children's taste for **a primary palette**, introduce the color in accessories and towels that can be **easily changed**.

Keep medicines and cleaners **under lock and key**.

Reduce the risk of scalding by opting for **a mixer instead of separate hot and cold faucets**.

resources

Alchemy Glass & Light
3143 South La Cienega
Los Angeles, CA 90016
310-836-8631
Glass sinks.

American Standard
1 Centennial Ave
Piscataway, NJ 08855
732-980-3000
www.americanstandard.com
Tubs, sinks, toilets.

Aquarius by Praxis Industries
Box 460, Industrial Park
Savannah, TN 38372
800-443-7269
Acrylic/fiberglass bath units.

Bed, Bath & Beyond
620 Avenue of the Americas
New York, NY 10011
212-255-3550
www.bedbathandbeyond.com
Everything for bed and bath.

Bloomingdales
1000 Third Avenue
New York, NY 10022
212-705-2000
www.bloomingdales.com
Department store; 24
locations nationwide.

The Conran Shop
407 East 59th Street
New York, NY 10022
212-755-9079
www.conran.com
Cutting-edge design.

Crate & Barrel
646 N Michigan Avenue
Chicago, IL 60611
800-996-9960
For a retailer near you, call
800-927-9202
www.crateandbarrel.com
Good-value accessories.

Elkay Mfg Co.
2222 Camden Court
Oak Brook, IL 60523
630-574-8484
www.elkay.com
Sinks, faucets.

Gemini Bath & Kitchen Products
1501 E. Broadway
Tucson, AZ 85719
520-770-0667
www.geminibkp.com
Showers, sinks.

Gerber Plumbing Fixtures Corp.
4600 West Touhy Ave
Chicago, IL 60712
847-675-6570
www.gerberonline.com
Toilets, bidets, faucets.

Heritage Marble of Ohio
7086 Huntley Road
Columbus, OH 43229
614-436-1464
Custom-made marble, onyx,
and granite fixtures.

Hold Everything
1309–1311 Second Avenue
New York, NY 10021
212-879-1450
www.williams-sonomainc.com
Everything for storage.

HydraBaths
2100 South Fairview St
Santa Ana, CA 92704
714-556-9133
www.hydrabaths.com
Whirlpools, steam cabinets.

Hydro Systems
50 Moreland Road
Simi Valley, CA 93065
805-584-9990
www.hydrosystem.com
Whirlpools, bathtubs,
showers, shower pans.

IKEA
Potomac Mills Mall
2700 Potomac Circle
Suite 888
Woodbridge, VA 22192
For a store near you, call
800-254-IKEA
www.ikea.com
Home basics at great prices.

Interbath
665 N. Baldwin Park Blvd
City of Industry, CA 91746
626-369-1841
www.interbath.com
Shower systems.

Jacuzzi Whirlpool Bath
2121 North California
Boulevard, Suite 475
Walnut Creek, CA 94596
925-938-7070
www.jacuzzi.com
Whirlpools, shower systems.

Kallista
2446 Verna Ct
San Leandro, CA 94577
510-899-6680
www.kallistainc.com
All kinds of fixtures.

Kohler Co.
444 Highland Drive
Kohler, WI 53044
800-4-KOHLER
www.kohlerco.com

MAAX
600 Rte Cameron
Ste-Marie-de-Bce
Que, CAN G6E 1B2
418-387-4155
Showers, tubs, whirlpools.

Macy's
800-BUY-MACY
www.macys.com
Department store;
locations nationwide.

Marble Madness
1430 S. Mint St
Suite C
Charlotte, NC 28703
704-343-2458
www.marblemadness.com
Mosaic sinks, stone
mirror frames.

Mirolin Industries Inc.
60 Shorncliffe Road
Toronto, Ontario
CAN M8Z 5K1
416-231-9030
Showers, tubs, shower
enclosures.

Neiman Marcus
For a store near you, call
888-888-4757
For mail order, call
800-825-8000
www.neimanmarcus.com
Department store;
31 locations nationwide.

PS Craftsmanship Corp.
1040 Jackson Ave
Long Island City
NY 11101
718-729-3686
Wooden lavatories,
vanities, bathtubs.

Restoration Hardware
935 Broadway
New York, NY 10011
212-260-9479
www.restorationhardware.
com
Not just hardware; funky
furnishings and accessories.

Sears, Roebuck
800-MY-SEARS
www.sears.com
Leading retailer of home
products and services
through catalog, retail
outlets, and online store.

Royal Baths Mfg Co.
14635 Chrisman Road
Houston, TX 77039
281-442-3400
www.royalbaths.com
Whirlpools, shower bases,
shower seats, toilets.

Sherle Wagner
60 East 57th St
New York, NY 10022
212-758-3300
www.sherlewagner.com
Luxurious fixtures and
accessories.

Swan Corp.
One City Center, 23rd floor
St Louis, MO 63101
314-231-8148
www.theswancorp.com
Shower systems, solid
surfaces.

Toto USA
1155 Southern Road
Morrow, GA 30260
770-282-8686
www.totousa.com
Toilets.

Waterworks
185 Steele St
Denver, CO 80206
800-998-2284
www.waterworks.com
Fixtures, tiles.

Whitehaus Collection
589 Orange Ave
Westhaven, CT 06516
800-527-6690
www.whitehaus
collection.com
Specialty bathroom products.

credits

Key: ph=photographer, a=above, b=below, r=right, l=left, c=center.

All photography by Chris Everard unless otherwise stated.

Front jacket Front jacket ph Chris Everard/New York City apartment designed by Marino + Giolito; **page 1** interior designer Alan Tanksley's own apartment in Manhattan; **2** ph Debi Treloar/Susan Cropper's family home in London, www.63hlg.com; **3** New York City apartment designed by Marino + Giolito; **4r** Simon Crookall's apartment in London designed by Urban Salon ; **5** ph Jan Baldwin/David Gill's house in London; **6–7** ph Henry Bourne/Dan and Claire Thorne's town house in Dorset designed by Sarah Featherstone; **8** both Fred Wadsworth's flat in London designed by Littman Goddard Hogarth; **9l** an apartment in Paris designed by Bruno Tanquerel; **9r** Simon Brignall & Christina Rosetti's loft apartment in London designed by David Mikhail Architects; **10l** a house in London designed by Carden & Cunietti; **10r** Andrew Wilson's house in London designed by Azman Owens; **11** both Vicente Wolf's home on Long Island; **12l** Monique Witt and Steven Rosenblum's apartment in New York, designed by Mullman Seidman Architects; **12–13 & 13c** ph Andrew Wood/a house near Antwerp designed by Claire Bataille and Paul ibens; **13r** Heidi Wish & Philip Wish's apartment in London designed by Moutarde & Heidi Wish; **14al** ph Ray Main/Client's residence, East Hampton, New York, designed by ZG DESIGN; **14ar** a house in London designed by Carden & Cunietti; **14bl** Andrew Wilson's apartment in London designed by Azman Owens; **14br** New York City apartment designed by Marino + Giolito; **15l** ph Andrew Wood/Roger Oates and Fay Morgan's house in Eastnor; **15r** ph Alan Williams/Richard Oyarzarbal's apartment in London designed by Urban Research Laboratory; **16l** John Minshaw's house in London designed by John Minshaw; **16r** Henry Bourne/Linda Trahair's house in Bath; **17l** Stephan Schulte's loft apartment in London; **17c** ph Andrew Wood/ Roger and Suzy Black's apartment in London designed by Johnson Naylor; **17r** ph Andrew Wood/house in London designed by Bowles and Linares; **18l** an apartment in New York designed by David Deutsch & Sidnam Petrone Gartner Architects; **18r** One New Inn Square, a private dining room and home of chef David Vanderhook, enquiries +44-(0)20-7729 3645; **19l** ph Ray Main/Jonathan Reed's apartment in London, lighting designed by Sally Storey, design director of John Cullen Lighting; **19ar** Michael Nathenson's house in London; **19br** Simon Brignall & Christina Rosetti's loft apartment in London designed by David Mikhail Architects; **20l** ph Jan Baldwin/Peter & Nicole Dawes' apartment, designed by Mullman Seidman Architects; **20r** a house in Hampstead, London designed by Orefelt Associates; **21l** an apartment in Paris designed by Bruno Tanquerel; **21ar** Jan Baldwin/Constanze von Unruh's house in London; **21br** architect Nigel Smith's apartment in London; **22a** Richard Hopkin's apartment in London designed by HM2; **22b** ph Jan Baldwin/art dealer Gul Coskun's apartment in London; **23al&bc** Heidi Wish & Philip Wish's apartment in London designed by Moutarde & Heidi Wish; **23ac** Hudson Street Loft designed by Moneo Brock Studio; **23ar** Freddie

Daniells' apartment in London designed by Brookes Stacey Randall; **23bl** Suze Orman's apartment in New York designed by Patricia Seidman of Mullman Seidman Architects; **23br** ph Jan Baldwin/Christopher Leach's apartment in London; **24a** Richard Hopkin's apartment in London designed by HM2; **24b** New York City apartment designed by Marino + Giolito; **25** Pemper and Rabiner home in New York, designed by David Khouri of Comma; **26** designed by Mullman Seidman Architects; **27** both ph Alan Williams/Gail & Barry Stephens' house in London; **28a** Monique Witt and Steven Rosenblum's apartment in New York, designed by Mullman Seidman Architects; **28bl** Heidi Wish & Philip Wish's apartment in London designed by Moutarde & Heidi Wish; **28br** Michael Nathenson's house in London; **29al** a house in Paris designed by Bruno Tanquerel; **29ar** Suze Orman's apartment in New York designed by Patricia Seidman of Mullman Seidman Architects; **29b** Mark Kirkley & Harumi Kaijima's house in Sussex; **30a** Alison Thompson & Billy Paulett's house in London designed by Stephen Turvil Architects; **30bl** a house in London by Seth Stein; **30br** ph Debi Treloar/Ian Hogarth's family home; **30–31a** Richard Oyarzarbal's apartment in London designed by Jeff Kirby of Urban Research Laboratory; **31a** a house in Hampstead, London designed by Orefelt Associates; **31b** Freddie Daniells' apartment in London designed by Brookes Stacey Randall; **32** ph Andrew Wood/ Johanne Riss' house in Brussels; **33al** New York City apartment designed by Marino + Giolito; **33ar** Vicente Wolf's home on Long Island; **33bl** Simon Brignall & Christina Rosetti's loft apartment in London designed by David Mikhail Architects; **33br** Paul Brazier & Diane Lever's house in London designed by Carden & Cunietti; **34–35** Calvin Tsao & Zack McKown's apartment in New York designed by Tsao & McKown; **36l** Stephan Schulte's loft apartment in London; **36r** Ian Chee of VX design & architecture; **37l** Monique Witt and Steven Rosenblum's apartment in New York, designed by Mullman Seidman Architects; **37r** Freddie Daniells' apartment in London designed by Brookes Stacey Randall; **38a** John Barman's Park Avenue Apartment; **38bl** ph Alan Williams/Hudson Street Loft designed by Moneo Brock Studio; **38br** Sera Hersham-Loftus' house in London; **39l** Gomez/ Murphy Loft, Hoxton, London designed by Urban Salon ; **39r** One New Inn Square, a private dining room and home of chef David Vanderhook, enquiries +44-(0)20-7729-3645; **40al** a house in Hampstead, London designed by Orefelt Associates; **40bl** ph Debi Treloar/family home, Bankside, London; **40r** ph Debi Treloar/a house by Knott Architects in London; **41l** ph Andrew Wood/Johanne Riss' house in Brussels; **41c** ph James Morris/the Jackee' and Elgin Charles House in California's Hollywood Hills, designed by William R. Hefner AIA, interior design by Sandy Davidson Design; **41r** Hilton McConnico's house near Paris; **42l** ph Tom Leighton/lofts in the old centre of Amsterdam of Annette Brederode, painter & dealer/collector of antiques and 'brocante' and Aleid Röntgen-Brederode, landscape architect; **42r** ph Tom Leighton; **43l** ph Tom Leighton/ Roxanne Beis' home in Paris; **43r** Sera Hersham-Loftus' house in London; **44bl** a house in

Hampstead, London designed by Orefelt Associates; **44ar** Frazer Cunningham's house in London; **44br** a house in Paris designed by Bruno Tanquerel; **45a both** a house in London designed by Helen Ellery of The Plot London; **45b** ph Tom Leighton; **46al** a house in Paris designed by Bruno Tanquerel; **46bl** ph Tom Leighton; **46r, 47l & 47ar** ph Debi Treloar/Kristiina Ratia and Jeff Gocke's family home in Norwalk, Connecticut; **47br** Emma & Neil's house in London, walls painted by Garth Carter; **48 & 48–49** Alison Thompson & Billy Paulett's house in London designed by Stephen Turvil Architects; **49b** ph Jan Baldwin/a house in New York designed by Brendan Coburn and Joseph Smith from Coburn Architecture; **50l** a house in Hampstead, London designed by Orefelt Associates; **50r** an apartment in New York, designed by Mullman Seidman Architects; **51** Pemper and Rabiner home in New York, designed by David Khouri of Comma; **52** main Central Park West Residence, New York City designed by Bruce Bierman Design; **52 inset** an apartment in New York, designed by Mullman Seidman Architects; **52–53** Fifth Avenue Residence, New York City designed by Bruce Bierman Design;

53bl Yuen-Wei Chew's apartment in London designed by Paul Daly Design Studio; **53ar&br** Ben Atfield's house in London; **54l** ph Debi Treloar/Paul Balland and Jane Wadham of jwflowers.com's family home in London; **54r** Monique Witt and Steven Rosenblum's apartment in New York, designed by Mullman Seidman Architects; **55** ph Debi Treloar/Victoria Andreae's house in London; **56l** ph Debi Treloar/a house by Knott Architects in London; **56ar** ph Debi Treloar/Vincent & Frieda Plasschaert's house in Brugge, Belgium; **56br** ph Debi Treloar/Catherine Chermayeff & Jonathan David's family home in New York, designed by Asfour Guzy Architects; **57a** ph Debi Treloar/family home, Bankside, London; **57b** ph Debi Treloar; **58al** ph Debi Treloar/a family home in Manhattan, designed by architect Amanda Martocchio and Gustavo Martinez Design; **58bl** ph Debi Treloar/The Swedish Chair—Lena Renkel Eriksson; **58r** Richard Hopkin's apartment in London designed by HM2; **58–59** ph Debi Treloar; **59ar** Catherine Chermayeff & Jonathan David's family home in New York designed by Asfour Guzy Architects; **59br** Simon Crookall's apartment in London designed by Urban Salon.

Architects and designers whose work is featured in this book

Alan Tanksley, Inc
212-481-8456
Page 1.

Amanda Martocchio, Architect
189 Brushy Ridge Road
New Canaan, CT 06840
Page 58al.

**Annette Brederode and
Aleid Röntgen-Brederode**
Lijnbaansgracht 56d
1015 gs Amsterdam
Page 42l.

Asfour Guzy Architects
212-334-9350
easfour@asfourguzy.com
Pages 56br, 59ar.

Azman Owens Architects
+44-(0)20-7739-8191
www.azmanowens.com
Pages 10r, 14bl.

Bowles and Linares
+44-(0)20-7229-9886
Page 17r.

Brookes Stacey Randall
+44-(0)20-7403-0707
www.bsr-architects.com
Pages 23ar, 31b, 37r.

Bruce Bierman Design, Inc.
212-243-1935
www.biermandesign.com
Pages 52 main, 52–53.

Bruno Tanquerel
+33-1-43-57-03-93
Pages 9l, 21l, 29al, 44br, 46al.

Carden Cunietti
+44-(0)20-7229-8559
www.carden-cunietti.com
Pages 10l, 14ar, 33br.

Christopher Leach Design Ltd
+44-(0)7765-255566
mail@christopherleach.com
Page 23br.

Claire Bataille and Paul ibens
+32-3-231-3593
Fax: +32-3-213-8639
Pages 12–13, 13c.

Coburn Architecture
718-875-5052
www.coburnarch.com
Page 49b.

Constanze von Unruh
+44-(0)20-8948-5533
www.constanzeinteriorprojects.com
Front jacket, page 21ar.

Coskun Fine Art London
+44-(0)20-7581-9056
www.coskunfineart.com
Page 22b.

David Khouri
Comma
212-420-7866
www.comma-nyc.com
Pages 25, 51.

David Mikhail Architects
+44-(0)20-7377-8424
www.davidmikhail.com
Pages 9r, 19br, 33bl.

David Vanderhook
+44-(0)20-7729-3645
Pages 18r, 39r.

Dive Architects
+44-(0)20-7407-0955
www.divearchitects.com
Pages 40bl, 57a.

Garth Carter
Specialist interiors painter
+44-(0)7958-412953
Page 47br.

Gustavo Martinez Design
212-686-3102
gmdecor@aol.com
Page 58al.

Heidi Wish
+44-(0)20-7737-7797
Pages 13r, 23al, 23bc, 28bl.

Helen Ellery
The Plot London
+44-(0)20-7251-8116
www.theplotlondon.com
Pages 45a both.

Hilton McConnico
+33-1-43-62-53-16
hmc@club-internet.fr
Page 41r.

HM2
+44-(0)20-7600-5151
andrew.hanson@harper-mackay.co.uk
Pages 22a, 24a, 58r.

Johanne Riss
+32-2-513-0900
www.johanneriss.com
Pages 32, 41l.

John Barman Inc.
212-838-9443
www.johnbarman.com
Page 38a.

John Minshaw Designs Ltd
+44-(0)20-7258-0627
Page 16l.

Johnson Naylor
+44-(0)20-7490-8885
brian.johnson@johnsonnaylor.co.uk
Page 17c.

jwflowers.com
+44-(0)20-7735-7771
www.jwflowers.com
Page 54l.

Knott Architects
+44-(0)20-7263-8844
www.knottarchitects.co.uk
Pages 40r, 56l.

Kristiina Ratia Designs
203-852-0027
Pages 46r, 47l & 47ar.

Littman Goddard Hogarth
+44-(0)20-7351-7871
www.lgh-architects.co.uk
Pages 8, 30br.

Marino + Giolito
212-675-5737
marino.giolito@rcn.com
Pages 3, 14br, 24b, 33al.

Mark Kirkley
+44-(0)1424-812613
Page 29b.

Michael Nathenson
+44-(0)20-7431-6978
www.unique-environments.co.uk
Pages 19ar, 28br.

Moneo Brock Studio
+34-661-340-280
www.moneobrock.com
Pages 23ac, 38bl.

Mullman Seidman Architects
212-431-0770
www.mullmanseidman.com
Pages 12l, 20l, 23bl, 26, 28a, 29ar,
37l, 50r, 52 inset, 54r.

Nigel Smith
+44-(0)20-7278-8802
n-smith@dircon.co.uk
Page 21br.

Orefelt Associates
+44-(0)20-7243-3181
orefelt@msn.com
Pages 20r, 31a, 40al, 44bl, 50l.

Paul Daly Design Studio Ltd
+44-(0)20-7613-4855
www.pauldaly.com
Page 53bl.

Reed Creative Services Ltd
+44-(0)20-7565-0066
Page 19l.

Roger Oates
Rugs and Runners Mail Order
Catalogue: +44-(0)1531-631611
www.rogeroates.com
Page 15l.

Sally Storey
John Cullen Lighting
+44-(0)20-7371-5400
Page 19l.

Sandy Davidson Design
Fax: 320-659-2107
SandSandD@aol.com
Page 41c.

Sarah Featherstone
Featherstone Associates
+44-(0)20-7490-1212
www.featherstone-associates.co.uk
Pages 6–7.

Sera Hersham-Loftus
+44-(0)20-7286-5948
Pages 38br, 43r

Seth Stein Architects
+44-(0)20-8968-8581
www.sethstein.com
Page 30bl.

Sidnam Petrone Gartner Architects
212-366-5500
www.spgarchitects.com
Page 18l.

Stephen Turvil Architects
+44-(0)20-7639-2212
turv@space1.demon.co.uk
Pages 30a, 48, 48–49.

Susan Cropper
www.63hlg.com
Page 2.

The Swedish Chair
+44-(0)20-8657-8560
www.theswedishchair.com
Page 58bl.

Tsao & McKown
212-337-3800
Fax: 212-337-0013
Pages 34–35.

Urban Research Lab
+44-(0)20-8709-9060
www.urbanresearchlab.com
Pages 15r, 30–31a.

Urban Salon Architects
+44-(0)20-7357-8000
Pages 4r, 39l, 59br.

Vicente Wolf Associates, Inc.
212-465-0590
Pages 11 both, 33ar.

VX design & architecture
ianchee@vxdesign.com
Page 36r.

William R. Hefner AIA
323-931-1365
www.williamhefner.com
Page 41c.

ZG DESIGN
631-329-7486
www.zgdesign.com
Page 14al.

index